THE GROWTH OF
FLORIDA

THE GROWTH OF
FLORIDA

Edward Riley

CHARTWELL
BOOKS, INC.

This edition published in 2007 by

CHARTWELL BOOKS, INC.
A Division of
BOOK SALES, INC.
114 Northfield Avenue
Edison, New Jersey 08837

ISBN-13 978-0-7858-2212-7
ISBN-10 0-7858-2212-7

© 2007 Compendium Publishing, 43 Frith Street, London, Soho, W1V 4SA, United Kingdom

Cataloging-in-Publication data is available from the Library of Congress

Printed and bound in China
Design: Ian Hughes/Compendium Design

Page 2: Sunset in Miami's Art Deco district. Florida has an eclectic range of architecture, from Colonial and Antebellum houses, to opulent Venetian-inspired mansions, set in a sub-tropical environment.

Page 4: With a history that can be traced back to the sixteenth century, Key West was once the favorite haunt of pirates and wreckers. Now known for its Bohemian culture, this is the most southerly place to live in the United States.

Contents

Introduction

A panoramic view of Downtown Miami and Biscayne Bay in the early 1990s showing a coastline that has been transformed into a modern urban metropolis.

Introduction

Extending out toward Cuba and the Bahamas and flanked by the Atlantic Ocean and the Gulf of Mexico, Florida is the southernmost state of the continental United States. Covering an area of over 58,000 square miles, it has a growing population in excess of 15,000,000 and is perhaps best known as a sun-drenched tourist destination of palm trees and beaches, theme parks and golf courses. Attracting tens of millions of tourists each year, it is, in fact, America's most visited state, but behind the modern day sand and sunshine is a fascinating history.

The earliest human inhabitants of Florida are thought to have been hunter-gatherers who occupied the area at least 12,000 years ago. Due to the much lower sea level of the time, the Florida peninsula was then more than twice its present size. Over the centuries these indigenous peoples developed complex cultures and began to trade with other natives in the area that is modern-day south-eastern America. By the time the first Europeans arrived in Florida there were an estimated 350,000 people belonging to a variety of different tribes and unaffiliated villages.

Modern, written, records of Florida begin with the arrival of the Spanish explorer Juan Ponce de Leon in 1513. Ponce de Leon made landfall on the north-east coast on April 2, 1513, and named the land *La Florida,* possibly due to the abundant plant life of the area or in honor of the fact that he had arrived during the Spanish

Easter festival of Pascua Florida. In 1521, Ponce de Leon returned with the 200 settlers, fifty horses, and the intention of founding a new colony. Though the first effort to establish a Spanish presence in Florida was thwarted by repeated attacks of the native people, Hernando de Soto led a doomed treasure hunting expedition through the area in 1539 and a further attempt to start a colony (in the area of modern day Pensacola) was made in 1559 by Tristan de Luna y Arellano. However, this too was abandoned in 1561.

By this time the area was beginning to draw the interest of other European powers and in 1564 the Frenchman, Rene Goulaine de Laudonniere, established Fort Caroline at the mouth of the St. Johns River, in the area that is now Jacksonville. This French activity spurred the Spanish into action and the next year, 1565, saw the founding of San Augustin (St. Augustine) by Pedro Menendez de Aviles. St. Augustine remains to this day and is the oldest continuously inhabited European settlement in the United States.

The following years saw an escalation in hostilities between the competing European powers in the region. In 1565, de Aviles captured Fort Caroline from the French and renamed it San

RIGHT: One of the earliest maps of Florida, drawn in the late sixteenth century by Theodor de Bry for a series on great voyages. In this somewhat inaccurate map of the area, Cuba is the most recognizable feature to modern eyes.

Mateo. Two years later Dominique Gourgues recaptured the fort and slaughtered the Spanish inhabitants. The village of St. Augustine was attacked and burned by the English privateer Sir Francis Drake in 1586.

This conflict continued to be played out over the next few decades as both the English and the French sought to push back the boundaries of Spanish control in the region. Colonel James Moore, with the aid of Creek Indian allies, attacked and destroyed the town of St. Augustine in 1702. However, they were unable to capture the attendant fort of Castillo de San Marcos. Undeterred, in 1704 Moore began a campaign of burning Spanish missions in north Florida and killing many native people allied to the Spanish. In 1719, the French captured the twenty-one year old Spanish town of Pensacola. The English founded their southernmost colony, Georgia, in 1733, thus putting them on the Spanish doorstep. From here

BELOW: One of the major threats that faced the earliest European colonists in Florida were the frequent attacks on their settlements by Native-Americans, as seen in this 1563 illustration.

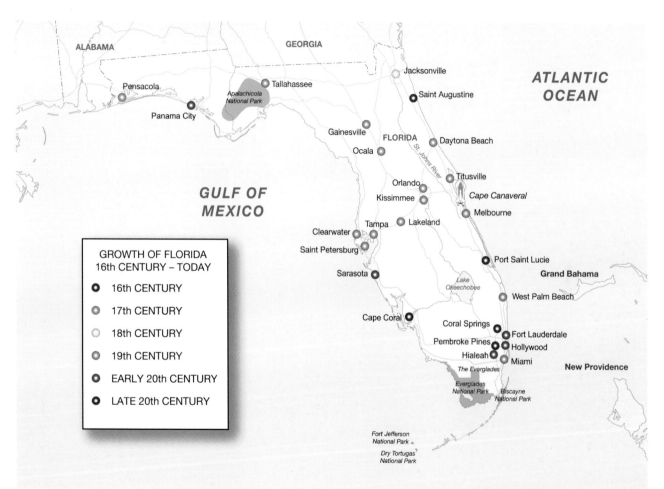

ALABAMA

GEORGIA

ATLANTIC OCEAN

Pensacola

Tallahassee

Jacksonville

Apalachicola National Park

Saint Augustine

Panama City

GULF OF MEXICO

Gainesville

FLORIDA

Daytona Beach

Ocala

St. Johns River

Titusville

Orlando

Cape Canaveral

Kissimmee

Melbourne

Tampa

Lakeland

Clearwater

Saint Petersburg

Port Saint Lucie

Grand Bahama

Sarasota

Lake Okeechobee

West Palm Beach

Cape Coral

Coral Springs

Fort Lauderdale

Pembroke Pines

Hollywood

Hialeah

Miami

The Everglades

New Providence

Everglades National Park

Biscayne National Park

Fort Jefferson National Park

Dry Tortugas National Park

GROWTH OF FLORIDA
16th CENTURY – TODAY

- 16th CENTURY
- 17th CENTURY
- 18th CENTURY
- 19th CENTURY
- EARLY 20th CENTURY
- LATE 20th CENTURY

A view of two early European cottages in the historic district of St. Augustine. The town is America's oldest colonial settlement and the historic district is full of old buildings reflecting its links to the past.

a further attack on Castillo de San Marcos was launched in 1740, resulting in a month-long siege. Despite the assault proving unsuccessful, it indicated a growing Spanish vulnerability in Florida.

The British gained control of Florida (at that time the region extended only as far south as modern-day Gainesville) in 1763 when they exchanged it for the recently captured Havana. When the Spanish evacuated, the province was left practically empty. St. Augustine was a fledgling town of no more than 500 buildings and Pensacola was just a small military town. The British split Florida into two parts: East Florida, with its capital sited at St. Augustine and West Florida with its capital at Pensacola. They then set about mapping a great deal of their new territory and a concerted attempt was made to entice settlers to the region. Nevertheless, British rule was to last for a mere twenty years.

Although both the Florida colonies stayed loyal to the British during the American War of Independence (1776-83), the Spanish took advantage of the conflict to recapture parts of West Florida, including Pensacola in 1781. When the revolutionary war ended, Florida was returned to Spanish rule under the terms of the Treaty of Paris.

Following the British example, the Spain began to offer extremely attractive free land packages to attract people to Florida. Colonists began to pour in from both Spain and the United States, including many escaped slaves who were keen to find a place where their former masters could not reach them. During this time, the United States Army carried out a number of incursions into Spanish Florida, including the Andrew Jackson led campaign

LEFT: The Old State Capitol in Tallahassee. Construction of the original brick capitol building was completed in 1845 and this structure remains the core of the Old Capitol to the present day. Major renovation was carried out on the building in 1902 and further improvements were made in 1923, 1936, and 1947. The modern Capitol Complex, including House and Senate chambers and offices, along with a twenty-two-storey executive office building was completed in 1977. The top of the high-rise office block can be seen behind the dome of the Old State Capitol that now houses the Department of State's Museum of Florida History.

BELOW The Ritz Plaza, National, and Delano hotels lie to the south of the Art Deco District of Miami Beach and echo its style. The 1930s and 1940s saw the construction of many Art Deco buildings in the area and this distinctive architectural style remains synonymous with Miami Beach.

against the Indians of 1817–18 that would later become known as the First Seminole War. On February 22, 1819, the United States and Spain signed the Adams-Onis Treaty, the terms of which ceded control of Florida to the U.S. in return for the country renouncing all claims to Texas. The terms of the treaty took effect from July 10, 1821.

Andrew Jackson returned to Florida in 1821 to oversee the new territorial government on behalf of the United States. East and West Florida were merged onto one, although a large area of what was then West Florida was annexed to the Orleans and Mississippi Territories. In 1824, a new capital was established at Tallahassee, midway between the two old capitals of St. Augustine and Pensacola. Tallahassee remains the state capital of Florida to this day.

The population of Florida now began to increase dramatically as more immigrants arrived from Virginia, Georgia, and the Carolinas. This led to pressure being put upon the United States government to evict the native Indians from the land they occupied and precipitated the Second Seminole War (1835–42). Led by Osceola, an estimated 4,000 Native-American warriors waged an effective guerrilla campaign against a far greater force of United States Army troops. The U.S. government, under President Andrew Jackson, spent more than twenty million dollars fighting the Seminoles. The war led to the deaths of more than 1,500 soldiers and countless Native-Americans and American civilians. By 1842, most of the surviving Indians had been moved, "voluntarily" or otherwise, to lands west of the Mississippi and a small number had retreated into the Everglades.

By 1840, the population of Florida exceeded 54,000, almost half being slaves. On March 3, 1845, Florida became the twenty-seventh state in the United States and by 1850 the population had swollen to over 187,000. Following the victory of Abraham Lincoln's Republican Party in the 1860 presidential election, the state seceded from the Union on January 10, 1861. During the Civil War that followed, Florida suffered far less than several other southern states. Although most of Florida's coast was captured, Tallahassee was the only southern capital east of the Mississippi to avoid invasion and the only major battle fought on the state's soil was the southern victory at the Battle of Olustee near Lake City.

After the north's victory in the war, Tallahassee was occupied by federal troops on May 10, 1865, and Florida was readmitted to the Union on July 25, 1868. The latter part of the nineteenth century saw a growth in both industry and agriculture in the state, driven in large part by the increasing number of railroads that were being built by entrepreneurs like Henry Flagler and Henry B. Plant. The origins of this expansion lay in the 1855 Internal Improvement Act that offered cheap, or in some cases free, public land to investors involved in transportation. This allowed the likes of Plant and Flagler to not only construct railroads, but to also build sumptuous hotels near their lines. The result was an influx of tourists from the northern territories and a much larger market for

RIGHT: A 1942 postcard of Florida featuring the Bok Tower, sandy beaches, the Everglades, and other tourist attractions of the state. Colorful postcards such as this were common in the 1940s and 1950s as Florida actively promoted itself as a tourist destination.

Greetings from FLORIDA "The Land of Sunshine"

© CURT TEICH & CO., INC.

the citrus industry, as it was now possible to transport freshly picked produce to places like New York and Philadelphia in less than a week.

During the 1920s, the population of Florida came close to a million for the first time and the state's economy boomed. However, the success was to prove short-lived. By 1926, the real-estate bubble had burst and the economy was further damaged by the severe hurricanes of 1926 and 1928. By the time the Great Depression began to sweep through the nation, the economic decay in Florida was already well underway and was further exacerbated in 1929 when an invasion of Mediterranean fruit flies severely disrupted the citrus industry.

Nevertheless, an upturn in the state's fortunes were not far away. Toward the end of the 1930s, the first theme parks began to emerge in Florida including Cypress Gardens near Winter Haven in1936 and Marineland near St. Augustine in 1938. In 1971, Florida welcomed the mouse: the first part of Walt Disney World Resort, The Magic Kingdom, was opened near Orlando and transformed of the Orlando area into a world-renowned holiday destination that now boasts a huge array of theme parks including Universal Orlando Resort, SeaWorld, and Wet 'n Wild.

The onset of World War II also had a beneficial effect on the economy of Florida. As the entire nation mobilized for war, the state became a key base for the American armed forces with the establishment of numerous naval, army, and air force stations. This in turn led to an accelerated program to update and improve the transport infrastructure of the state that would prove to be of great benefit to the tourism industry in the years following the war.

Florida was selected in 1949 as a test site for the United Sates embryonic missile programme and over the next decade Patrick Air Force Base, located near Cocoa Beach, and the Cape Canaveral launch site on the coast of Brevard County were built. The Space Race of the 1960s saw a huge growth in the industry and this area has since become collectively known as the Space Coast. The latter part of the twentieth century and the beginning of the twenty-first century has seen a steady growth in the population of Florida and a greater diversification in the economy of the area. Tourism and the citrus industry remain important, but these have been supplemented by more modern industries such as electronics, plastics, and international banking.

From its beginnings as a much fought-over European colony, Florida has developed into a modern American state that is internationally renowned and welcomes millions of tourists from all around the world every year. From peaceful keys once infested with pirates and lovely Art Deco hotels to the cutting-edge Kennedy Space Center and modern thrill rides, Florida is a magnificent adventure and has overcome a turbulent past to outshine the rest of the United States. While no volume can hope to comprehensively document the growth of such a rich and diverse area, we hope that this book provides a fascinating glimpse into how Florida has evolved and grown into America's Sunshine State.

LEFT: Cinderella's Castle at Walt Disney World in Orlando. The construction of Walt Disney World led to the Orlando area becoming a worldwide center of theme park tourism.

A Saturn V rocket on display outside the Vehicle Assembly Building at John F. Kennedy Space Center in Cape Canaveral. The aerospace industry is an important part of the modern Floridian economy and Florida remains the paramount location for the U.S. space programme. Indeed, all the manned spaceflights launched by the U.S. so far have blasted-off from the Kennedy Space Center.

Discovery and Colonization: 1513–1820

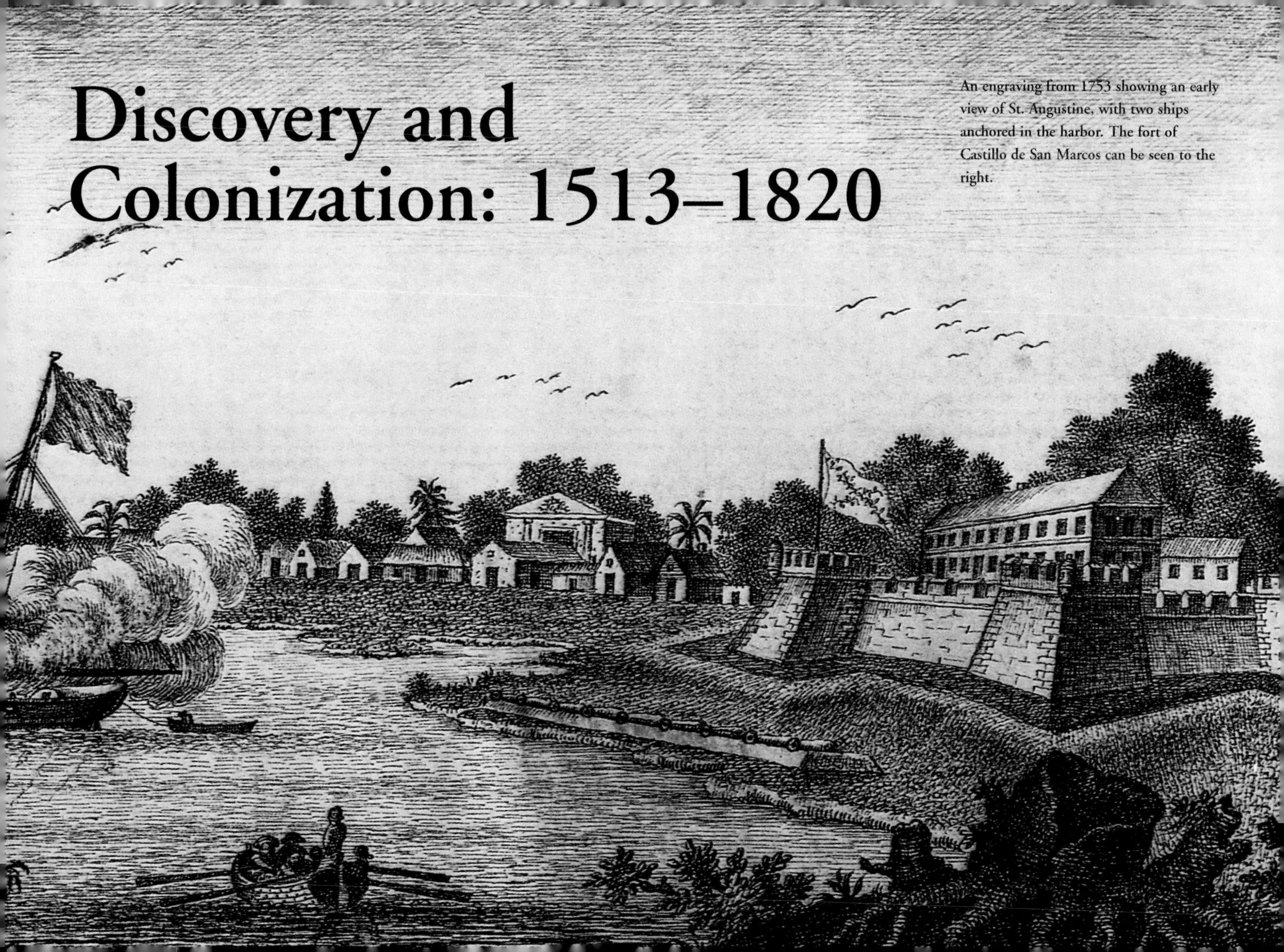

An engraving from 1753 showing an early view of St. Augustine, with two ships anchored in the harbor. The fort of Castillo de San Marcos can be seen to the right.

Discovery and Colonization: 1513–1820

As with most colonies in the "New World," Florida's early appeal was as a place where wealth could be found to enrich the coffers of the competing European powers. As well as being seen as a potential source of riches in its own right, the area was also an important link in the Gulf Stream trade route used by Spanish treasure ships returning from more southern colonies. Naturally, the other great European powers of the time—France and England—were keen to usurp Spanish influence in the area and lay claim to any wealth for themselves, which led to frequent high-seas clashes. As well as the threat posed by rival nations, shipping was also in danger of attack from pirates such as the infamous Blackbeard, who operated out of the Caribbean and preyed upon the east coast of Florida during the seventeenth and eighteenth centuries.

Despite European politics, unfriendly natives, and high-seas drama, European settlers gradually came to Florida: the French notably founded the first successful settlement of La Caroline in 1564 before being wiped out by the Spanish. Spain's first permanent colony, St. Augustine, dates to the following year. The early Spanish colonists brought with them the first cattle and horses to arrive in North America, as well as their religion (the Jesuits began to arrive in 1566) and European diseases, to which the Native-Americans succumbed in devastating numbers. One of the mainstays of the Spanish colonial blueprint for Florida was the founding of missions to convert the indigenous population to Christianity and thereby pacify them. The Spanish also had a tolerant attitude toward runaway slaves, which encouraged many to flee from the British Carolinas to Florida. Probably in part to antagonise the British, the Spanish established Fort Mose (near St. Augustine) in 1738, the first independent black community in North America.

The first two centuries or so of Florida's colonial history were riven with warfare and infighting. Settlements were small and often hard pressed. It was after the English gained control of Florida in 1763, that the region saw the largest influx of European settlers when around 1,400 people, under the leadership of Dr. Andrew Turnbull, established a colony at New Smyrna, along the west bank of the Indian River in 1768. However, the colony—like so many before it—struggled and English rule in Florida was to last for only twenty years.

Although the second period of Spanish government of Florida was in many ways more successful, increased conflict with the United States eventually led to the Spanish ceding Florida to the U.S. in 1821.

RIGHT: This 1591 hand-colored engraving by Theodor de Bry shows the layout of Fort Caroline, established by the Frenchman René Goulaine de Laudonniere in 1564 at the mouth of the St. Johns River.

OCCIDENS.

25

LEFT: The establishment of La Caroline by the French led the Spanish to build and fortify a colony at St. Augustine, seen here in this map from 1588.

BELOW: Not all the natives encountered by the early settlers were unfriendly; Spanish settlers arriving by ship can be seen being escorted to St. Augustine by Native-Americans in this illustration from *The Unknown New World*, printed in Amsterdam, Holland, in 1673. The nascent Castillo de San Marcos can be seen in the background.

Castillo de San Marcos

Although the fort had an important role as the protector of both St. Augustine and the Spanish fleets returning to Europe, for over a century the fortifications of Castillo de San Marcos were simple wooden structures. In 1672, the Spanish began construction of the more substantial stone fort that still stands today and is a designated National Monument. It is the oldest surviving masonry and only extant seventeenth century fort in North America and provides an excellent example of the "bastion system" of fortification.

LEFT: A cannon facing out to sea from the Castillo de San Marcos. From the gun deck the Spanish cannons were able to fire on targets up to three miles away. To the left can be seen the watchtower located on the fort's northeast bastion. Manned twenty-four hours a day, this tower was used to look out for enemy ships.

RIGHT: An aerial view of Castillo de San Marcos, giving a marvellous view of the "bastion system" of fortification that was prevalent at the time of its construction.

PREVIOUS PAGE LEFT: A view of the courtyard at Castillo De San Marcos; storage rooms and guard stations can be seen on the right. In the top left, under the rampart leading up to the gun deck, is "La Necessaria," a tidal-flush sewage system.

PREVIOUS PAGE RIGHT: After the U.S. took control of Florida in 1821, Castillo de San Marcos was renamed Fort Marion and used mainly as a storage depot and military prison. This picture from the 1860s shows a structure that has become rather run-down, perhaps reflecting the less than vital status of the fort at this time.

RIGHT: The moat and walls of Castillo de San Marcos: the walled area across the moat was known as the "covered way" because it shielded defending soldiers from enemy fire. The sloped base of the wall, the "glacis" was designed to protect the fort from cannon fire.

LEFT: Known as the Oldest House, or the Gonzalez-Alvarez House, this building is thought to be the oldest surviving house in the United States. The site has been occupied since the 1600s and the present building dates to the early 1700s. Originally the one-storey home of Spanish artilleryman Tomas Gonzalez, a second storey was added to the building during the English occupation of 1763–83.

RIGHT: An interior view of the Gonzales-Alvarez House. Since 1893, the house has been open to visitors, displaying artifacts of the Spanish, British, and American occupations of St. Augustine and showing how the residents lived. In 1970, the U.S. Department of the Interior designated the house a National Historic Landmark.

LEFT: At the north end of St. George Street, St. Augustine, stand these city gates, once the only entrance to the enclosed city. Built in 1739, the gates were constructed of stone while the rest of the city wall was wooden. Outside the wall was a deep ditch filled with water. The entrance to the gates was via a drawbridge that was raised at night.

RIGHT: Situated on Rattlesnake Island, with a commanding position over Matanzas Inlet, Fort Matanzas was built between 1740 and 1742 by the Spanish following a blockade of St. Augustine by Governor James Oglethorpe of Georgia that led to a thirty-nine day siege. Oglethorpe took advantage of the fact that the southern mouth of the Matanzas River can be used as a back entrance to St. Augustine and thus avoided the primary defences at Castillo de San Marcos.

LEFT: The Old Wooden Schoolhouse is believed to be the oldest surviving wooden structure in the U.S. Built some time before 1788, the schoolhouse is constructed of pest-resistant red cedar and cypress timbers secured with wooden pegs and cast-iron spikes. The huge chain that can be seen wrapped around the building was added in 1937 to anchor it to the ground during hurricanes.

RIGHT: While De Luna's attempt to found a colony here in 1559 failed, Pensacola was successfully established in 1696 by three hundred men under Don Andres d'Arriola. A small fort called San Carlos was built with a church and several dwellings nearby. This 1778 plan of Pensacola shows the fort bounded on three sides by the developing suburban areas.

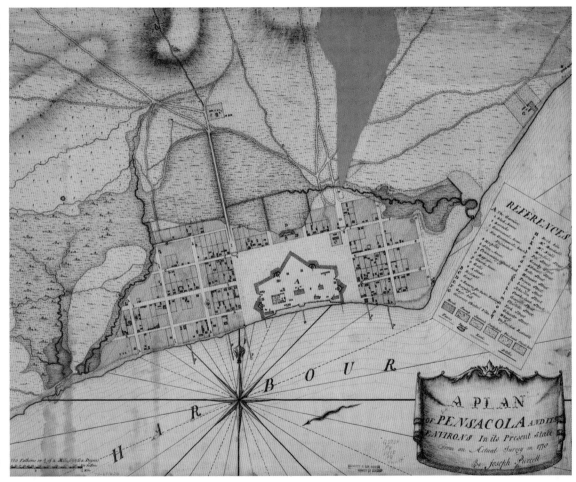

LEFT: Churches formed an integral part of the early colonies. The Basilica Cathedral of St. Augustine still incorporates the 1797 parish church and is one of the oldest Roman Catholic religious buildings in the U.S.

ABOVE: Originally built in 1797 as a one-storey home and store for a Spanish merchant, the Ximenez-Fatio House, on Aviles Street in St. Augustine, had a second storey added prior to its conversion into a boarding house during the mid-nineteenth century.

Standing in the grounds of what is now the Timucuan Ecological and Historic Preserve, the Kingsley Plantation is the oldest plantation house in Florida. Situated at the northern end of Fort George Island and built in 1798, it takes its name from the wealthy plantation owner Zephenia Kingsley who moved here in 1814.

LEFT: Slave Quarters at the Kingsley Plantation. Even though Zephenia Kingsley was considered a liberal thinker in his day (indeed he married a freed slave, Anna Jai) and despite the relative modesty of his home compared to those of other plantation owners, the contrast between the luxury of the plantation house and the very basic homes of the slaves who worked in the fields is vast.

RIGHT: The Prince Murat House is one of the oldest surviving colonial structures in St. Augustine. Built in the late eighteenth century, it takes its name from its most famous inhabitant, Prince Achille Murat, the nephew of Napoleon Bonaparte who is reputed to have lived in the house during the year of 1824.

The Julee Cottage on Zaragoza Street, Pensacola, is dedicated to the memory of the African-American freewoman, Julee Panton, who purchased this unusual "to the sidewalk" building in the early 1800s. Panton, who owned her own business and invested in real estate, loaned money to slaves so that they could buy their freedom. The cottage was later owned by a succession of free African-American women and today houses the Julee Cottage Black History Museum.

This rare example of French Creole colonial architecture, known as the Lavalle House is sited on East Church Street, Pensacola. Carlos Lavallé and Marianna Bonifay, a French widow who had fled from Santo Domingo during a slave revolt in the 1790s, built the house in the early 1800s.

Antebellum Florida: 1821–61

The increasing tensions between European Americans and Native-Americans, as well as the black slave population, led to the killing of nearly four hundred white settlers in Florida between December 1835 and April 1836, as seen in this contemporary sketch entitled *Massacre of the Whites by the Indians and Blacks in Florida.*

Antebellum Florida: 1821–61

The intertwined issues of the Seminole Wars and the drive to achieve statehood dominated the early part of the four decades between Florida becoming a territory of the United States and the beginning of the American Civil War. Plantations had already started to appear in Florida at this time and as more people from the older Southern plantation regions began to arrive, the pressure on the federal government to relocate the Native-Americans and free up their land for white settlers increased. The first attempt to achieve this goal peaceably was made by Territorial Governor William F. Duval as early as 1823. Duval met with the Seminoles and, along with the majority of their chiefs, signed the Treaty of Moultrie Creek that granted the Indians reservations in central Florida in return for their land in the north. Nevertheless, troubled flared up between white settlers and the Native-Americans almost as soon as the ink was dry and whites responded by lobbying for the Indians to be removed from Florida altogether. The Treaty of Fort Gibson sought to achieve this in 1833 by moving the Seminoles to land in Oklahoma. However, when the duplicitous nature of the treaty became apparent, it so outraged some of the Native-Americans that it precipitated the Second Seminole War that was to prove so costly.

Although the people of the territory were divided on the issue of statehood, with plantation owners generally in favor and smaller landholders less enthusiastic, as early as 1837 a bill was passed to achieve a referendum. The territory now needed to entice more settlers to raise its population. Steamboat travel was already established and railroads began to be built to improve the transportation infrastructure of Florida and thus encourage immigration. The cause of statehood was also greatly aided by the Florida Armed Occupation Act of 1842 that granted 160 acres of land in unsettled areas of Florida to anyone willing to bear arms to defend it for five years.

On July 4, 1845, Florida, along with Iowa, officially joined the United States and slavery became the dominant issue of the day. Most white Floridians of the time were not opposed to slavery and there was growing concern at the anti-slavery movement that was gaining momentum in the North. This issue was bought to a head in 1861 when, following Abraham Lincoln's victory in the presidential election, Florida seceded from the Union.

RIGHT: The Bulow Plantation Ruins Historic State Park, located three miles west of Flagler Beach, is part of a 4,675 acre site that was purchased in 1821 by Major Charles Bulow. The land was cleared by slaves and turned into a plantation with rice, cotton, and sugar cane fields. Bulowville, as it was known at the time, was abandoned following Indian attacks during the Seminole Wars.

ABOVE: A rare example, in Florida, of the French Creole High House (a Gulf Coast architectural style), the Barkley House, at 410 South Florida Blanca Street, Pensacola, was built by a prominent local merchant family in the mid-1820s. One of the oldest masonry houses in Florida, it has been restored and renovated recently and is now open to the public.

RIGHT: Wrecking, the practice of taking valuables from a shipwreck that has foundered near or close to shore, was a major industry in the Florida Keys throughout much of the nineteenth century. Believed to be the oldest building on Key West, the Wreckers Museum, on Duval Street, was originally built in 1829 as the home of the wealthy wreck captain, Francis B. Watlington.

Built in 1830 for William "Money" Williams, "The Columns" is Tallahassee's oldest surviving residential building. Although the story is undoubtedly apocryphal, local legend has it that Williams had a nickel baked in every brick of the building prior to its construction. The ghost of a Civil War widow called Rebecca is also rumored to haunt the house.

A view of the powder magazine at Fort Pickens. The fort is located at the western tip of Santa Rosa and was the largest of four (the others being Fort Barrancas, Fort McRee, and the Navy Yard) that were built to defend Pensacola Bay. Colonel William H. Chase of the Corps of Army Engineers supervised the fort's construction, by slave labor, which began in 1829 and was completed by 1834. The famous Apache chieftain, Geronimo, was imprisoned here between 1886 and 1888 and the fort remained in use by the U.S. Army up until 1947.

LEFT: This large, roomy manor house in Tallahassee was originally the home of General Richard Keith Call who had it built in the early 1830s prior to his appointment as governor of Florida in 1835. During his tenure he built the first railroad in the state, from Tallahassee to St. Marks (at the time an important port).

RIGHT: The First Presbyterian Church, on Park Avenue and North Adams Street, Tallahassee, was built in the late 1830s. As well as serving its intended function as a place of worship, the building was also used by early settlers as a barricaded fort during the Seminole Wars.

LEFT: The main house of the Goodwood Plantation, on the north-eastern edge of Tallahassee was built during the 1830s, at which time the plantation was a major producer of cotton and corn. The main house still retains many of its original features, including an impressive mahogany staircase. After years of neglect the plantation buildings are currently being restored.

BELOW: Fort Taylor stands at the tip of Key West. Construction of the three-storey, trapezoid-shaped fort that was built to defend what was then Florida's largest city, began in the mid-1840s, but was hampered by constant shortages of men and material as well as outbreaks of yellow fever. It eventually took twenty-one years to complete. The fort was modernized in 1898 during the Spanish-American war, resulting in the elimination of the top two stories to facilitate the installation of newer weapons. Fort Taylor was placed on the National Register of Historic Places in 1971 and in 1973 was designated a National Historic Landmark.

LEFT AND RIGHT: Two maps of Antebellum Florida, separated by a decade. The first (to the left) was drawn up by Joseph Goldsborough Bruff in 1846 and the second (right) comes from the annual report of the Surveyor General for 1856.

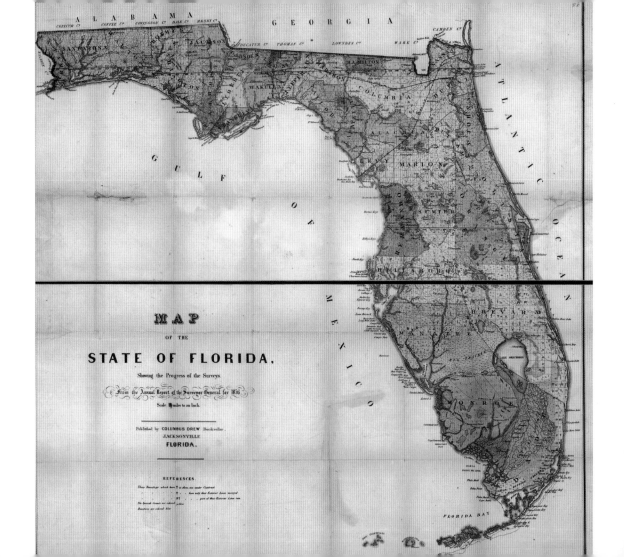

MAP

OF THE

STATE OF FLORIDA,

Showing the Progress of the Surveys.

From the Annual Report of the Surveyor General for 1856

Scale 9 miles to an inch.

Published by COLUMBUS DREW Bookseller,
JACKSONVILLE
FLORIDA.

REFERENCES.

Those Townships which have a dot in them are under Contract
T . . have only their Exterior Lines surveyed
PT . . . part of their Exterior Lines run
The Special Census are colored yellow
Donations are colored blue

An aerial view of Fort Jefferson located on the Dry Tortugas, a series of seven reef islands lying to the west of Key West. Originally planned to guard the Florida Straits with a garrison of 1,500 men and 450 cannon, work began on Fort Jefferson in 1845 and continued for the next thirty years, beset by many of the same problems that dogged the construction of Fort Taylor. Despite being the largest brick fortification in the U.S., Fort Jefferson was never fully completed and was never involved in any battle. During the Civil War it was occupied by Union forces and used as no more than a prison for captured deserters.

Built between 1845 and 1850 by Major Robert Gamble, this whitewashed mansion situated in Ellenton, on the Gulf Coast, is the only surviving antebellum house in southern Florida. Originally, the house stood on a 3,500-acre sugar plantation that was worked by just under 200 slaves. By 1856, Gamble found himself in financial difficulties and was forced to sell the house, its ground, and the surrounding plantation (including slaves) for $190,000.

63

Situated at the northern tip of Amelia Island (north-east of Jacksonville), Fort Clinch was built to guard the Cumberland Sound at the mouth of the St. Mary's River. The fort is an irregular brick pentagon with huge earthworks and five-foot-thick walls. It was built between 1847 and the early 1860s.

The Golden Age: 1862–1920

Now the Lightner Museum, this building was formerly the Alcazar Hotel, one of the many luxury hotels that were built by the railroad tycoon Henry Flagler during Florida's Golden Age.

The Golden Age: 1862–1920

During the Civil War Florida supplied roughly 15,000 troops to the Confederate Army while some 2,000 Floridians fought for the Union. The state was also a significant provider of food supplies, mainly livestock such as beef and pork, for the Confederates, leading the Union to blockade the whole state. When the northern states prevailed and the slaves were emancipated, Florida's economy was irrevocably changed. Plantation owners who had relied on slave labor to run their operations now found it difficult to make profits using hired help and much of the former plantation land was converted to farmland. However, some towns—Jacksonville and Pensacola for example—prospered as the demand for timber to rebuild the war-ravaged nation increased. In fact, while the economy in many areas of the country was in ruins, Florida was about to enter a Golden Age of expansion and affluence. Alongside established businesses such as logging and large-scale commercial agriculture, new industries such as cigar production began to appear, driven by the large number of Cuban immigrants that had begun to arrive in the state.

By the 1870s, wealthy tourists from the colder northern states were also flocking to the warmer climes of Florida. At first accommodated on steamboat tours of the rivers, the great railroad tycoons Henry Flagler and Henry Plant soon began the construction of the railroads and opulent hotels that would change the face of Florida. By 1890, the north of Florida and the east and west coasts were criss-crossed by railroads and by 1912 even the Florida Keys were joined to the mainland by rail.

The development of Palm Beach by Henry Flagler in the 1890s into an exclusive resort is a classic example of the new, vibrant Florida that emerged from the shadows of the Civil War.

RIGHT: The Dorr House on South Adam Street, Pensacola was built in 1871 by the widow of a lumber tycoon. Thought to be the last remaining example of Greek Revival architecture in West Florida, it is similar in style to the double gallery houses of New Orleans. The house now houses a museum replete with furnishings and memorabilia from the 1850s to 1890s.

ABOVE: John B. Stetson University was founded in 1883 by Henry A. DeLand and was originally called the DeLand Academy. In 1889, however, it was renamed in honor of John B. Stetson who was both a founding trustee of the university and a considerable contributor to its early finances. In 1900, the university opened its law school, the first in Florida and in 1960 it became the first white college in Florida to admit a black student. This photograph shows the Science Hall.

RIGHT: The following four pages contain panoramic maps of (in sequence) Lake City, Pensacola, and Tallahassee drawn in 1885 and Jacksonville drawn in 1893. These maps—beautiful in their own right—show some of the burgeoning cities of Florida during its golden age of expansion and prosperity.

THE BORUM HOUSE

PANORAMIC·VIEW·OF

LAKE CITY, FLA.

COUNTY-SEAT OF COLUMBIA-CO

1885.

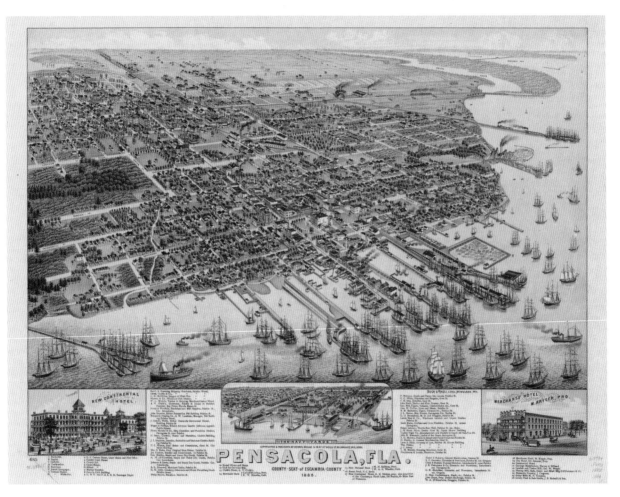

PENSACOLA, FLA.

COUNTY-SEAT of ESCAMBIA-COUNTY.

1885.

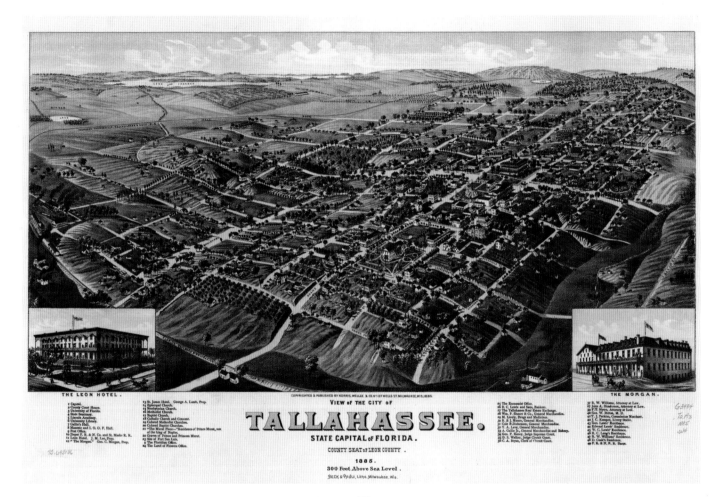

THE LEON HOTEL.

THE MORGAN.

COPYRIGHTED & PUBLISHED BY NORRIS, WELLGE & CO. N.º 127 WELLS ST. MILWAUKEE, WIS. 1885.

VIEW OF THE CITY OF

TALLAHASSEE.

STATE CAPITAL OF FLORIDA.

COUNTY SEAT OF LEON COUNTY.

1885.

300 Feet Above Sea Level.

BECK & PAULI, Litho, Milwaukee, Wis.

1 Capitol.
2 County Court House.
3 University of Florida.
4 State Seminary.
5 Lincoln Academy.
6 University Library.
7 Gallie's Hall.
8 Masonic and I. O. O. F. Hall.
9 Post Office.
10 Depot F. R. & N. Co. and St. Mark's R. R.
11 Leon Hotel. J. M. Lee, Prop.
12 "The Morgan." Geo. C. Morgan, Prop.

13 St. James Hotel. George A. Lamb, Prop.
14 Episcopal Church.
15 Presbyterian Church.
16 Methodist Church.
17 Baptist Church.
18 Catholic Church and Convent.
19 Colored Methodist Churches.
20 Colored Baptist Churches.
21 "The Murat Place,"—Residence of Prince Murat, son of the king of Naples.
22 Graves of Prince and Princess Murat.
23 Site of Fort San Luis.
9 The Floridian Office.
24 The Land of Flowers Office.

25 The Economist Office.
26 B. C. Lewis and Sons, Bankers.
27 The Tallahassee Real Estate Exchange.
28 Wm. P. Slusser & Co., General Merchandise.
29 M. Lively, Drugs and Medicine.
30 R. & J. Munro, General Merchandise.
31 Cole B. Dickenson, General Merchandise.
32 V. A. Levy, General Merchandise.
33 A. Gallie Jr., General Merchandise and Bakery.
34 Geo. P. Raney, Judge Supreme Court.
35 D. S. Walker, Judge of Circuit Court.
36 C. A. Bryan, Clerk of Circuit Court.

37 R. W. Williams, Attorney at Law.
38 John A. Henderson, Attorney at Law.
39 P. W. Myers, Attorney at Law.
40 Geo. W. Betton, M. D.
41 T. J. Perkins, Commission Merchant.
42 C. Kasper, Livery Stable.
43 Geo. Lewis' Residence.
44 Edward Lewis' Residence.
45 W. C. Lewis' Residence.
46 R. C. Long's Residence.
47 R. W. Williams' Residence.
48 R. Cook's Residence.
49 F. R. & N. R. R. Shops.

G.3484
To P.3
1885
.W4

JACKSONVILLE
FLORIDA

Standing over 115 feet tall, the Ponce de Leon Inlet Lighthouse has a beacon that can be seen up to nineteen miles out to sea. Built in 1887 to guard the hazardous entrance at the tip of the Daytona peninsula, it is now open to the public and has a small museum located in a former keeper's cottage at its base, which has been restored to its 1890s appearance.

Paddle steamers were a common sight around Florida from the days when they were used as troopships during the Seminole wars. As can bee seen in this photograph of Silver Springs, which dates to 1886, some of the state's earliest tourists arrived by steamer.

LEFT: Flagler College in St. Augustine was originally one of Henry Flagler's luxury hotels, the Ponce de Leon. Built between 1885 and 1888 it was heralded on its opening as "the worlds finest hotel."

RIGHT: The beautiful red wood of the Flagler College rotunda provides a rich canvas for pendant murals created by George W. Maynard and gives a feeling of the luxury enjoyed by guests at the former Ponce de Leon hotel.

LEFT: Henry Flagler built the Memorial Presbyterian Church in memory of his daughter Jennie Louise Benedict, who died in 1889. The church, which took less than a year to complete, is in the Venetian Renaissance Revival style and was modeled after St. Marks in Venice.

ABOVE: A Moorish-style dome and minarets rise above the trees at the Tampa Bay Hotel. The hotel was built in 1891 by the railroad magnet Henry B. Plant at a cost of over $2.5 million and was considered the foremost of the eight hotels that Plant built to anchor his rail line. The 511 rooms were the first in Florida to have electric lights and telephones. The building now houses part of the University of Tampa.

LEFT: Built in 1892 for the Lewis Bear Company, the Bear Block at 402–410 Palafox Place, Pensacola, is memorable for its striking Classical Revival details and decorative cast-iron balconies.

RIGHT: The Royal Poinciana Hotel in Palm Beach was a 2,000-room wooden hotel that opened in 1894. The six-storey, Georgian-style hotel was believed to be both the largest hotel and the largest wooden structure in the world at the time. Unfortunately, the majority of the building was destroyed by fire in 1935.

LEFT: The extension of Henry Flagler's Florida East Coast Railway to Miami marked the beginning of the meteoric growth of the city and of other resort communities nearby. This train arrived in Miami on April 15, 1896. A few months later the sleepy fishing village was incorporated as a city.

RIGHT: A 1900 map of Florida showing the rapidly expanding railroad network that was so vital to the economic growth of the state.

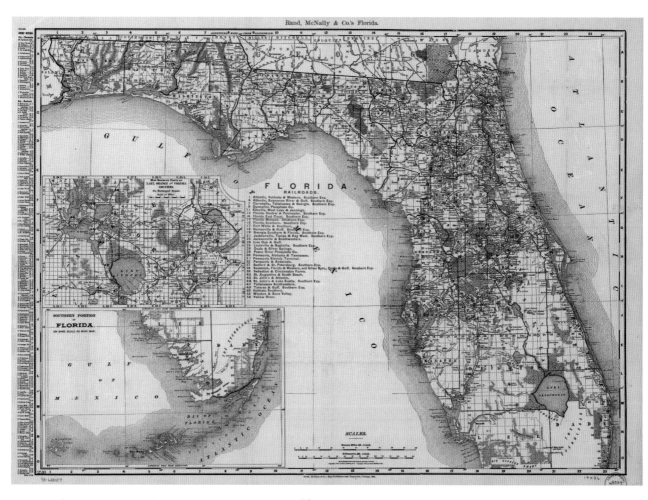

LEFT: Consisting of little more than three forts at the time of the Second Seminole War, by 1900 Fort Lauderdale had become a busy trading post. Stranahan House at 335 South-East Sixth Street, is the oldest surviving house in the modern city. Built by the pioneer Frank Stranahan in 1901, it served many functions including post office, trading post, and bank.

ABOVE: This fifty-five room Palm Beach mansion, known as "Whitehall" was built in 1902, at a cost of four million dollars, by Henry Flagler and given to his wife Mary Lily Kenan as a wedding present. The Flaglers used it as a winter residence, which they traveled to every year in one of their private railroad cars. In 1925, the building was converted to a hotel, but in 1959 Jean Flagler Matthews bought her grandfather's old mansion, restored it, and converted it into the Flagler Museum.

Two panoramic views Pensacola in 1909. The town's fortunes began to boom after the end of the Civil War when the region's timber was in much demand. By the beginning of the twentieth century Pensacola had grown out of recognition. Across the city timber money financed opulant houses and new civic buildings.

Founded on the shore of the St. John's River in 1822, by the end of the nineteenth century, Jacksonville was a successful and bustling transportation hub and the capital of the First Coast of Florida. This panoramic photograph shows the city in 1910.

Looking north from the Mugge Building over Tampa in 1913. Famous for its cigar manufacturers, the city is also appropriately the home of Henry Plant's amazing Moorish Tampa Bay Hotel (now the Henry B. Plant Museum). Up until Plant's railroad reached the city in 1880, it was a small and sleepy backwater town.

LEFT: A shack on Pigeon Key used by workers building the railroad bridge from South Florida out to the Florida Keys. The Overseas Railroad was the brainchild of Henry Flagler, but the project was beset by problems and the eventual cost was estimated at between twenty and forty million dollars. In spite of all the difficulties, the final link was completed in 1912 and it was widely known at the time as the "Eighth Wonder of the World." When the section of the railroad in the Middle Keys was partially destroyed by a hurricane on September 2, 1935, the Florida East Coast Railway could not afford to rebuild the destroyed sections, so the structure was sold to the State of Florida.

RIGHT: The facade of the former Pensacola Grand Hotel, now the Crowne Plaza Pensacola Grand Hotel. The building was constructed in 1912 as the L&N Railroad Depot.

A panoramic map of West Palm Beach, North Palm Beach, and Lake Worth just twenty-five years after Henry Flagler began buying up land and converting the area to a winter resort town. Along with other hotels both the Breakers (originally the Palm Beach Inn) and the Royal Poinciana can be seen.

NORTH PALM BEACH

LAKE WORTH

ATLANTIC OCEAN

LEFT AND ABOVE: Views of the front facade and an ornamental terrace in the gardens of Vizcaya museum. Built in 1916 as the winter residence of the millionaire industrialist James Deering, Vizcaya proved too costly to maintain after his death and was eventually sold, in 1952, to Dade County whereupon the house and its grounds were converted into a museum. Probably Florida's grandest residence in its heyday, Deering's wish was that Vizcaya should replicate a sixteenth century Italian estate and the mixture of styles on display in its opulent rooms, as well as the perfectly laid out formal gardens, certainly lend themselves to this impression.

The Depression and Beyond: 1921–60

Once one of the most magnificent homes in Palm Beach, Mar-A-Lago was built in 1927 by Joseph Urban and Marion Wyeth. The house, with its fifty-eight bedrooms and thirty-three bathrooms, were bought in 1985 by Donald Trump and converted into an exclusive private club.

The Depression and Beyond: 1921–60

The development and economic growth that symbolized Florida's Golden Age continued into the first half of the 1920s with land developers making fortunes and ever more tourists flocking to the state. With the arrival of the first affordable automobile, the Ford Model T (nicknamed the Tin Lizzie), less wealthy families than those who had previously been able to afford the trip began to make their way to Florida. Known as "Tin Can Tourists" they holidayed in the trailer parks that sprung up to cater for this new form of tourism.

The good times could not last forever though, and by the time the Great Depression hit in 1929, the economy in Florida was already struggling. But in 1933, Franklin D. Roosevelt was elected President and the era of the "New Deal" was ushered in. Florida benefited as thousands of young men were put to work improving the state's infrastructure. New schools and federal buildings were built, along with many of the state's parks and wildlife preserves.

While the New Deal helped reinvigorate Florida's businesses, entrepreneurs also had a hand in pulling the state back toward profitability. During the 1930s banking was given a boost by businessman Alfred DuPont, who was also largely responsible for kick-starting the paper industry in Florida. The citrus industry that had been hard-hit in the late 1920s and early 1930s also began to recover and was soon shipping fruit throughout the United States. During World War II Florida became an important training center for both the U.S. armed forces and those of her allies. Following the war the tourism industry began to boom again and Florida was once again on the up.

RIGHT: The City Hall of Opa-Locka at the junction of North-West Twenty-Seventh Avenue and North-West 135th Street, Miami. Inspired by *The Arabian Nights,* aviator Glenn Curtiss created the fantasy city of Opa-Locka during the boom times of the early 1920s. Consisting of around ninety buildings, it was known at the time of its construction as the "Baghdad of Dade County."

ABOVE: Built in 1927, the Bridge of Lions replaced a wooden toll bridge that connected downtown St. Augustine with Anastasia Island. The bridge was placed on the National Register of Historic Places in 1982, currently it is undergoing an extensive renovation program.

RIGHT: The Spanish-style Congregational Church in Coral Gables. George E. Merrick, the founder of the City of Coral Gables, donated the land for the church, and construction began on November 2, 1923. The completed building was dedicated on Palm Sunday, April 5, 1925.

The first decades of the twentieth century were a boom time for Miami, which grew from a small trading town to one of the United States most popular vacation destinations within a few short years, as the following three photographs show. To cater to the millions who flocked to enjoy the year round sun and sand, the town grew at an intense pace. On Miami Beach, development was especially rapid after a bridge joined the island to the mainland in 1913. The 1925 photograph of boats anchored off the shore, shows the steel frames of ever larger hotels under construction.

inter Bathers at Miami...Jan., 1921.

LEFT: Colorful marble paving surrounds Ca' d'Zan, built in 1924–26 by John Ringling, founder of the Ringling Brothers Circus. The villa, which overlooks Sarasota Bay, was originally intended to combine certain architectural features drawn from two of his wife Mabel's favorite Venetian hotels: the Danieli and the Bauer-Grünwald. Its Venetian name translates as "House of John." When John Ringling died in 1936, he willed his collection of art, the mansion, and its grounds to the state of Florida. Ten years later the Ringling Museum opened its doors to the public.

RIGHT: Light from stained glass windows in the ceiling shines onto the floor of the magnificent ballroom in Ca' d'Zan, The ceiling paintings are by the Hungarian-born artist Willy Pogany, a popular book illustrator who also designed sets for the Ziegfeld Follies and the New York Metropolitan Opera.

LEFT: The Freedom Tower, on Biscayne Boulevard, is a fine example of the Neo-Classical style that was popular in Miami during the boom years of the early 1920s. When it was built in 1925, the tower served as the home for the now-defunct *Miami News*. During the 1960s it gained the name Freedom Tower when it was used as the reception center for Cubans fleeing the Castro regime. The tower is seen here illuminated on the eve of the 2003 Latin Grammy music awards.

RIGHT: The Orange Blossom Special train leaving a station on February 3, 1925. The passenger train was a Pullman (luxury sleeping car) extra fare train that carried wealthy society people from Pennsylvania Station in Manhattan to the posh resorts along the east coast of Florida.

LEFT: The Don Cesar hotel, nicknamed "the Pink Lady," is located in St. Pete Beach and has a chequered history. Thomas Rowe built the hotel between 1925 and 1928 at a cost of $1.2 million. During World War II it was sold to the army for $450,000 and converted into a military hospital. At the end of 1945 it was converted into a Veterans Administration Regional Office. In 1969, the Veterans Administration moved out and the building was vacant for a few years, until it was sold to William Bowman Jr. in 1972. The Holiday Inn franchise owner reopened the Don Cesar in November 1973.

RIGHT: The Bok Singing Tower, decorated with images of Floridian wildlife, houses a fifty-three-bell carillon. The tower and 128-acres of woodland gardens were gifted to the American public in 1930 by Edward W. Bok, an immigrant from Holland who went on to become a successful publisher. The Historic Bok Sanctuary has now been expanded to cover 250 acres. Bok's grave can be found at the base of the Singing Tower.

Daytona's association with racing began in 1903 when the first organized speed trials took place on Ormond Beach. The trials continued on the beach until 1935—seen here is part of a crowd of over 50,000 who came to see Sir Malcolm Campbell shatter his own automobile speed record on February 22, 1933. This was one of the five times that Campbell broke the record at Daytona, the last being in September 1935.

An aerial view of the Joseph P. Kennedy estate on Palm Beach. The oceanfront property was bought in 1933 by Joseph P. Kennedy Sr. as a vacation spot and later became his son's winter White House.

The modern Daytona International Speedway was opened in 1959 and signaled the end of racing on the beach. The most famous race held here annually is the Daytona 500, which is so popular that the 110,000 seats are inevitably sold out a year in advance.

Miami Beach Art Deco

Art Deco was a movement in the decorative arts that grew to influence architecture. The movement had its foundations in the Exposition Internationale des Arts Décoratifs et Industriels Modernes held in Paris in 1925. Ocean Drive on Miami's South Beach has an array of buildings that were built during the 1930s and 1940s in various Art Deco styles and the surrounding area is also full of fine examples of this distinctive architectural style. When constructed, the majority of these Art Deco buildings were white, but during the 1980s the designer Leonard Horowitz covered around 150 buildings in the colorful pastel shades that are seen today.

A major reason that so many of these buildings still stand is that in 1976 Barbara Capitman set up the Miami Design Preservation League, which continues to campaign for preservation, protection, and promotion of these landmarks to this day.

RIGHT: An Art Deco-style lifeguard station on the beach in South Miami Beach. The pastel coloring and style of the hut echo those of the buildings on Ocean Drive.

FAR RIGHT: The Breakwater Hotel was designed by Anton Skislewicz and built in 1939. The hotel has a nautical theme with the central tower reminiscent of a ship's funnel and the rooftop railings resembling those on deck.

A classic view of Miami's South Beach
showing a street of pastel-colored Art Deco
buildings with sandy beach and palm trees
in the foreground.

Two views of the Colony Hotel, the first (LEFT) in its original white incarnation and the second (RIGHT) a more recent, night-time, view showing the blue pastel shades that were added in the 1980s.

LEFT: Built in 1939, the Century Hotel was designed by the renowned Art Deco architect Henry Hohauser. The hotel retains much of its original charm and in recent years has been the recipient of the Miami Design Preservation League's award for outstanding facade preservation.

RIGHT: The Waldorf Towers, built in 1937, lit up at night showing one of Ocean Drive's more memorable landmarks, the ornamental lighthouse atop the hotel.

The Annie Pfeiffer
Chapel (LEFT) and the E.
T. Roux Library (RIGHT)
at Florida Southern
College in Lakeland.
The college has the
distinction of housing
the largest collection of
buildings designed by
the celebrated architect
Frank Lloyd Wright.
Work began on the
campus in 1938 with a
plan for eighteen
buildings to be
constructed.
Unfortunately, by the
time Wright died in
1959 only seven of the
projected buildings had
been fully built, though
eventually a further five
were completed. Despite
this the campus certainly
has the light, airy feel
that Wright sought to
achieve.

Seen here in 1951, Silver Springs is
Florida's longest operating tourist
attraction, having been welcoming visitors
since 1878. From the shore of the planet's
biggest artesian spring, the town's famous
Jungle Cruises still run glass-bottomed
boat tours.

Modern Florida: 1961–Today

The glass- and steel-dominated skyline of
modern Jacksonville as seen from across
the St. Johns River. First founded as
"Cowford" in 1791, Jacksonville has grown
into the epitome of a modern city.

Modern Florida: 1961–Today

In the latter part of the twentieth century, Florida continued to thrive and the population increased rapidly as more and more people, attracted by the year-round sunny weather and low taxes, moved in. In 1950, the population of Florida—at that time just under three million—was the twentieth highest in the U.S., but by 2000 the number of Florideans had risen to over fifteen million and Florida had become the fourth most populated state. Florida also became home to a large proportion of retirees; the over-65s now make up almost twenty percent of the state's total population.

Tourism remains crucial to the economy in Florida with over seventy-five million visitors every year contributing to state finances, attracted by cheaper air-fares around the world coupled with the development of theme parks like Walt Disney World and Universal Orlando Resort as well as the Kennedy Space Center. The downside of the rapid rise in population and the vast number of tourists is the strain that this places on the environmental resources of the state. In recent times the conservation of Florida's native fauna and the preservation of its natural habitat has become an area of grave concern. Although it has always been prone to hurricanes, the development of coastal areas has also meant that the area is increasingly susceptible to the destructive power of these natural disasters. Indeed, the hurricane season in 2004 alone caused over forty billion dollars of damage.

While there are certainly many challenges facing the state in the twenty-first century, Florida finds itself in robust health and continues to be renowned world-wide as the "Sunshine State."

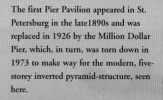

The first Pier Pavilion appeared in St. Petersburg in the late1890s and was replaced in 1926 by the Million Dollar Pier, which, in turn, was torn down in 1973 to make way for the modern, five-storey inverted pyramid-structure, seen here.

Kennedy Space Center

Situated on Merritt Island in Brevard County, midway between Miami and Jacksonville, the John F. Kennedy Space Center (K.S.C.) covers an area of 219 square miles and employs around 17,000 people. As well as being a NASA launch facility K.S.C. also has a popular visitor center, which makes the site one of the major tourist destinations in Florida.

A group of six United States rockets on display at the Spaceport U.S.A. museum in the John F. Kennedy Space Center.

An aerial view of the Vehicle Assembly Building; this is where spacecraft are assembled and readied for flight. The launch pads can be seen in the distance.

The launch of Freedom Seven from
Launch Complex Five on May 5, 1961.
Freedom Seven was the Redstone rocket
that carried Commander Alan Shepard,
America's first human in space. Launch
Complex Five is now a museum containing
all of the original equipment used to
launch the Mercury-Redstone rockets.
Tours can be arranged through the
Kennedy Space Center Visitor Center.

RIGHT: A view of the mission control
center used by NASA during Project
Mercury, the United States' first successful
manned spaceflight program, which ran
from 1959 through to 1963.

ABOVE: Visitors to the space center in 1974 were able to get a preview of the joint U.S.–Soviet manned spacecraft mission planned to take place in mid-1975. On display are full-scale models of the American Apollo and Russian Soyuz spacecraft as they would appear during their docking exercises.

RIGHT: The Space Shuttle *Discovery* approaching the Rotating and Fixed Service Structures on Launch Pad 39B after rollout from the Vehicle Assembly Building in April 2005. The shuttle sits atop the Mobile Launcher Platform and is transported by the Crawler-Transporter underneath.

LEFT: Constructed between 1979 and 1982, the Seven Mile Bridge (on the left) was one of the longest bridges in the world when it first opened. Extending from Key Vaca, in the Middle Keys, to Little Duck Key in the Lower Keys it runs parallel to the old bridge built by Henry Flagler in 1912.

ABOVE: The plaza and facade of the public library at the Miami-Dade Cultural Center was designed by Philip Johnson in 1982. As well as the library, the center, at 101 West Flagler Street, Miami, also houses an art gallery.

141

The three-tiered Bank of America Tower (originally known as the Centrust Tower) is one of the most prominent landmarks in the Miami skyline. Built in the 1980s the forty-seven-storey office tower is renowned for its after-dark illuminations.

RIGHT: The space-age looking Miami Metromover is an automated public transportation system that was first opened in 1986. The driverless carriages run on an elevated track and serve the downtown area of Miami. The system is one of five in the U.S., one of the others being the Jacksonville Automated Skyway Express.

Everglades National Park

Despite having an area of over 1.5 million acres, the Everglades National Park covers only twenty percent of the original Everglades area. Home to an abundance of rare and endangered species such as the American crocodile and the Florida panther, the park is the largest subtropical wilderness in the United States. Such is its importance, both globally as well as nationally, that it has been designated as an International Biosphere Reserve, a World Heritage Site, and a Wetland of International Importance.

LEFT: Shark Valley is located on the northern boundary of the Everglades, in the Shark River Slough. The sixty foot observation deck seen here is a great place from which to view the varied wildlife of the area such as alligators, white-tailed deer, and wading birds.

ABOVE: An aerial view of the Ten Thousand Islands area of Everglades National Park at sunset. Despite their name, the Ten Thousand Islands number only in the hundreds; nonetheless this labyrinth of mangrove islets and waterways, south of Everglades City, is home to an abundance of marine species.

Eco Pond, near the Flamingo Visitor Center, at the southern tip of the park is a freshwater pond that boasts a wide variety of wading birds, song-birds, and other wildlife.

LEFT: The Sunshine Skyway Bridge, with its distinctive taxicab yellow cabling, soars high above Tampa Bay. Built of steel and concrete it is the world's longest cable-stayed concrete bridge. Work began on the bridge in 1982 and was finished in 1987 at a cost of $244 million.

ABOVE: Built at a cost of $57 million and opened in August 1987, the Tampa Bay Performing Arts Center is the largest of its kind south of the John F. Kennedy Center for the Performing Arts in Washington, D.C. Situated on the east bank of the Hillsborough River, the center houses five separate theaters within its nine-acre site.

Florida Hurricanes

Florida has a long history of hurricanes and tropical storms. Indeed, on average, one in ten of the hurricanes that arise in the North Atlantic makes landfall in the state and between 1871 and 1990 Florida has been hit by over seventy. These days the National Hurricane Center in Miami monitors hurricane activity and can detect any threat long before it arrives. Although this early warning can and does save many lives the damage caused is still devastating at times.

LEFT: The Labor Day Hurricane of 1935 caused widespread damage throughout the Florida Keys and killed over 400 people. Seen here is the Florida East Coast Emergency Relief train that was blown off its tracks by the winds.

ABOVE: The remains of Montego Bay, a housing development in Dade County wrecked by Hurricane Andrew in 1992. Despite causing twenty-five billion dollars worth of damage, making it the most costly natural disaster to hit the U.S. at the time, Hurricane Andrew was responsible for only fifteen deaths in Florida.

Left: Fort Pickens in Pensacola Bay shown flooded after Hurricane Ivan swept through the area on September 16, 2004.

Hurricane Katrina, that went on to devastate New Orleans, first made landfall in Florida. Seen here a parking lot in Fort Lauderdale battered by high winds of over eighty miles per hour blowing rain and sand.

The 76,000-capacity Alltel Stadium, in downtown Jacksonville is the home of the NFL Jacksonville Jaguars. Opened on August 18, 1995, at a of cost $135 million, the stadium also plays host to a range of other events such as rock concerts and monster truck shows.

ABOVE: The centerpiece of the Holocaust Memorial sited, appropriately at 1933–1945 Meridian Avenue, Miami Beach. Miami Beach is home to one of the world's largest populations of Holocaust survivors; a committee of these survivors were the driving force behind the memorial that was designed by Kenneth Treister and opened in February 1990.

RIGHT: The blue, curved dome of the state-of-the-art Florida Aquarium is one of the outstanding features on the waterfront of Tampa City Center. Opened in 1995, the aquarium houses displays of marine life from around the world.

The evening skyline of Miami. The epitome of modern Florida, the city boasts a population of two million and is a business and tourist center with a distinct and laid back culture that is influenced by Latin America.

Picture Credits
Photographs supplied by the Prints and Photographs division of the Library of Congress unless otherwise specified. Map page 11 by Mark Franklin.

CORBIS IMAGES
Thanks to Toby and Katie at **Corbis** who supplied most of the color images—specifically. Page 2 Joseph Sohm; ChromoSohm Inc.; 4-5 Bob Krist; 6-7 Joseph Sohm; ChromoSohm Inc.; 10 Archivo Iconografico, S.A.; 12 Peter Finger; 14 Joseph Sohm; Visions of America; 15 Patrick Ward; 17 Lake County Museum; 18 Blaine Harrington III; 20-21 Ross Pictures; 22-23; 25 Archivo Iconografico, S.A.; 27 Bettmann; 28 Reinhard Eisele; 29 James L. Amos; 30-31 Raymond Gehman; 32-33 David Sailors; 35 Nik Wheeler; 36 Lee Snider/Photo Images; 37 Lee Snider/Photo Images; 38 Nik Wheeler; 40 Dave G. Houser; 42-43 Gerald French; 44 Lee Snider/Photo Images; 45 Nik Wheeler; 48-49; 51 Raymond Gehman; 53 Patrick Ward; 55 Raymond Gehman; 62 Bob Krist; 63 Lee Snider/Photo Images; 64-65 Robert Holmes; 66-67 Dave G. Houser; 70 Lake County Museum; 75 Lake County Museum; 78 Wolfgang Kaehler; 79 William A. Bake; 81 Patrick Ward; 83 Lake County Museum; 84 Bettmann; 86 Tony Arruza; 87 Patrick Ward; 92 Buddy Mays; 93 Dave G. Houser; 96 Peter Finger; 97 Tony Arruza; 98-99 Steve Starr; 101 Tony Arruza; 102 Nik Wheeler; 103 Lee Snider/Photo Images; 108 Patrick Ward; 109 Patrick Ward; 110 Daniel Aguilar/Reuters; 111 Bettmann; 112 Photo Company/zefa; 114-115 Bettmann; 116 Bettmann; 117 Duomo; 118 Patrick Ward; 119 Klaus Hackenberg/zefa; 120-121 Joseph Sohm; Visions of America; 123 Wisser Bill Sygma; 125 Patrick Ward; 130-131 Gerald French; 132-133 Dave G. Houser; 134 Dave G. Houser; 135 ; 136 Bettmann; 137 Roger Ressmeyer; 138 Bettmann; 139 NASA/epa; 140 Bob Krist; 141 Tony Arruza; 142 Tony Arruza; 143; 144-145 Patrick Ward; 145 Phil Schermeister; 146-147 Dave G. Houser; 148 Raymond Gehman; 149 Richard Klune; 150 Bettmann; 151 Raymond Gehman; 152 Joe Skipper/Reuters; 153 Mike Theiss/Jim Reed Photography; 154-155 Charles W Luzier/Reuters; 156 Jan Butchofsky-Houser; 157 Lee Snider/Photo Images; 158-159 Murat Taner/zefa